MY PURPOSE IS

Annette M. Walls Flournoy

Copyright © 2020 Annette M. Walls Flournoy

All rights reserved. No part of this publication may be reproduced, distributed, or transmitted in any form or by any means, including photocopying, recording, or other electronic or mechanical methods, without the prior written permission of the publisher, except in the case of brief quotations embodied in critical reviews and certain other noncommercial uses permitted by copyright law.

ISBN-978-1-951300-04-3

Liberation's Publishing LLC
West Point, Mississippi
www.liberationspublishing.com

A very special thanks to Estella Walls

Acknowledgement

I would like to give an honor to my Heavenly Father in the person of My Lord and Savior Jesus Christ. And to my husband Darnell Flournoy

This book is dedicated to
My Children
My Grandchildren
In Remembrance of My
Mother Marie Fleeton

Contents

Introduction 11

Forgiveness 15

Reality Check 33

Bargain 49

My First Healing 63

Fall From Grace 71

South Bend 85

Rainbow 93

Don't Give Up 103

ABOUT THE AUTHOR 115

INTRODUCTION

As I attempt to bring to you my life changing greetings, I first need to let you know that I am going to introduce to you the one who is in charge of my mind altering state. In the King James version Philippians 2:5 states: Let this mind be in you, which was also in Christ Jesus. Now giving an honor to GOD who is the creator of all living being and who is the head of my life, I will dive right into this to let you know in the beginning God.

GOD being a spirit can do what he pleases. There is none above Him. Everything you do in life will always end back up to Him. You can't get past Him. He took a part of himself by the earth not being able to contain him, wrapped himself in some human flesh, placed it inside of a body that was made spotless, blameless, and put it inside of a virgin by the name of Mary.

Matthews 1:21 states: And she shall

bring forth a son, and thou shalt call his name JESUS: for he shall save his people from their sins. Not saying that you won't make mistakes because you will, but yes you can live without sin. Yes, we are all from the time that the first man Adam sinned by eating of a fruit that the Almighty GOD had instructed him not to eat of, has landed all of us to be born in sin and shaped in iniquity.

It caused us to be out of fellowship with the one who created all living things and all living beings. So that is why Jesus had to come to our rescue, being put to shame by being scorned, being beaten, and was crucified, He did die, He was buried, and was resurrected in order to put us all back into fellowship with the Almighty Creator of All Living Being.

Read Genesis Chapters one, two, and three as well as Matthews chapter one. Isaiah chapter fifty-three is another, just to name a few reference scriptures. In this we will learn that you can overcome all types of obstacles and accomplish the goal or goals that you set your mind to do. Because after all We can do all things through Christ Jesus who strengthens us.

Philippians 4:13. I do pray that in this your mind will continue to be in Christ so that whatever you're faced with in life you can achieve your highest form of accomplishment. Praying that you can relate to some of the things in here and know that you are not alone. And that by the time you are done with this, you will get up and start your journey.

FORGIVENESS

Forgiveness is to pardon or be pardon of one faults or mishaps, cancel a debt, and or to wipe the slate clean.

Mark 11:25-26 says it like this, and when you stand praying, forgive, if ye have ought against any: that your Father also which is in heaven may forgive you your sins. But if you do not forgive, neither will your Father which is in heaven forgive you your trespasses.

Be careful to forgive. See I know that there is a real GOD that can deliver and heal and can set free because there has been situations and times in my life that I have been backed up in corners even as a child up until adulthood that I know nobody got me out of those situations but GOD. I was raised to pray the Our Father Prayer as a child not knowing the meaning of it, but it did teach me some morals as far as what you are not supposed to do against God. You know the simples don't steal, don't lie, don't kill, treat people right, go to church type thing you know. And when you die you will go to heaven. But as I got older I later learned that it took a lot more than that. I learned that it was a name that I had to call on to be saved out of situations and that name was Jesus.

There is a scripture in Colossians 3:17 that states, And whatsoever ye do in word or deed, do it all in the name of the Lord Jesus, giving thanks to God and the Father by him. I've learned that I had to go though some sure enough, ups and downs and sicknesses and a whole mess of hurts and pains that I wouldn't want anybody else to go through. I've cried so many nights, I've experienced the pain of loneliness which it felt like a knife was stabbing me all over my body and would not wish that on my worst enemy.

No I don't have any enemies outside of imps amen. I had to learn how to do some fasting and praying hard and some forgiving in order to be brought up in the beauty of the person I am today. See I can forgive any person who has done me hurt because that's what has cause me to have many, many Victories amen. I'm talking about the kind of victories that had others saying things like, she's on welfare how she get this and that, how did she get that job, look at how her children are well mannered, how she get that education? how she overcame the streets, it's something different about her. Just to name a few. Well I was just plain ole Net Walls.

I will later on give you deep details on how good, bad, awful, and beautiful of the things that took place in my life. But for now this is still just an introduction to (My Purpose Is). Now people have this saying real bad that I forgive you but I won't forget, well let me remind you of something, that means truthfully you haven't forgave them, and I will say well, Jesus forgave me and dropped my sins in the sea of forgetfulness who are you to bring it up again. So I try to be somewhat mindful like that to the point of I do forgive and I can and will forgive any and everybody who caused me pain and do have a hard time remembering it, unless it's brought back to my attention and asked to be used as an illustration among family for a particular reason. Such as in family discussions or person to person to get things straight. I must say that I have a heart of forgiveness and I will apologize.

You have to have a heart of Forgiveness and a Repenting heart too amen. These two go hand and hand. Without these two I personally don't see how a person can survive mentally because it has a lot to do with your growth and development. There are so many things that comes with these two words, for one thing, the Blessings I have experienced by following after them and allowing my spirit to submit, that just blows my mind beyond belief.

When I would fall into a situation that needs attention such as, Example (when I fell into the hands of the enemy), this is where I would go to the Lord for understanding and His Word the Bible which in turn stands for:

B = BIBLICAL

I = INTELLIGENCE

B = BEYOND

L = LIBERAL

E = EDUCATION

This is where I also get this saying you can have all the knowledge in the world and no action than you are just an all knowing person doing nothing. So let's continue to move Beyond Liberal Education and look always to GOD's knowledge in every aspect of our life amen, amen. Now it has been many, many days that I have sat here trying to figure out what I was going to write about. Saying that wasn't anybody going to read it and people wasn't going to understand where I was coming from, so I just kept on prolonging and contemplating what I was going to write about.

So as I begin to write the Lord begin to

deal with me about me and the truth of my journey, which is (My Purpose Is).

My main purpose for writing this is to help somebody else know that whatever it is you are facing in life, regardless if it attacked you or you brought it upon yourself, first Forgive Yourself and Repent and know that there is a real Big GOD that sits high and looks low at whatever you are going through.

He will come beside you and help you through it and help you to overcome it. If it's mental issues, cancer, drugs, homelessness, hunger, hurt, just to name a few and/or anything that tries to rob you of your dignity, your confidence, your self-respect, and your accomplishments. That's who and how GOD is. He will forgive you and give you back everything that the enemy stole from you even when you were a child up to adulthood because He Loves you just that much.)

First I must say that in order to be

forgiven, you must have the heart of forgiveness and a heart of repentance. I use this saying, how do I expect GOD to forgive me if I can't forgive you. In order for me to be forgiven I have to repent saying I'm sorry from deep within not to bring it up again. Now it's up to you to forgive me because I've done my part. And after I've asked you to forgive me it gives me a clearance to have a free spirit and mind to continue on with my day.

Now when I would go into prayer I would ask GOD if I was forgiven? There was as I believe to be a personal sign between me and him to let me know that I had been forgiven. I'm not talking about Him dying on the Tree, that goes without saying. But yes He would let me know that I had been forgiven. When you have a real personal relationship with him he will grant you what you ask.

Not looking for a sign but in order for my conscience to be clear after and if I've caused hurt to myself or someone, he would let me know by this particular thing after I pray for forgiveness. ABANDONED To be abandoned means to be left alone, forsaken, having to be deserted, to give up, to leave, or even cast off anything, place, or person. Isaiah 54:7 says it like this, For a small moment have I forsaken thee; but with great mercies will I gather thee.

Psalms 27:10 says it like this, When my mother and my father forsaken me, then the Lord will take me up. O. k. some time ago, there was an incident that happened to me and my siblings that left me with a longing for my maternal mother. At the age of eight I knew what happened but I just couldn't understand why it was happening. I later found out that it was for my good, but it still left me feeling like I was alone.

Although there was a lot of new type family members around me and the love and welcoming that was presented to me, I was still left with the feeling of why, which after a few years starting to grow a new type of feeling within me which grew into anger and frustration. Because as the years went by the longing got stronger because of the things that I was dealing with.

Starting off with being molested, getting beatings, and longing for my maternal mom. I start thinking about my surroundings and all the activities that I was involved in that I was like ok this is the way it's going to be so I might as well get used to it. But GOD. While in this particular situation, I had to deal with forgiving people. I had so much anger inside me that I wouldn't hardly talk to anybody.

I was hurt almost every day thinking about how I was left alone in this apartment along with my younger siblings at which I was the oldest at that time being only eight years old. I stayed mad all the time that people use to say to me even as a teenager, why don't you smile sometimes? Smile, smile for what, what was I supposed to be smiling about. Also what I knew about being mad, I was only eight. I don't know but the fact that I was left alone. You know how you tell somebody something and you would laugh behind it? Oh I can see somewhat why some wouldn't believe, because behind the pain that I would tell and talk about from time to time when I got a chance, I would be smiling or laughing to keep from crying even though I know they could see the water in my eyes. For instant, when I would get whooped or beat, I used to go get cleaned up, go into the kitchen and say to my little sister, oh momma thought that hurt. Knowing good well that it did.

Momma would say, oh you not gon cry while I was getting whooped on. I would just laugh afterwards to keep the pain inside. Which I believed it left me thinking I had mental issues, but that was not the case. That was to cover up the hurt which wasn't good because it led me in other directions when I got a little older that wasn't good for me, and when a certain ugliness presented itself to me that's the route I would take. Now this part of me being molested and touched happened before I got with my new family and also after I was placed with my new family. But I was mad because I'm wondering why we were left alone. Like momma you don't love me? What I do? Did I do something wrong? Like it was my fault that we were by ourselves. Where are my two younger brother and sister at?

You know, I didn't know what to do and how can I find mom and after I was with my new family I even packed my little purse with my doll, toothbrush, and some other stuff in it and ran away across the street to the park. This was the first time I call myself running away. I was only a child. I was confused. Let's back up before my adopted family.

This the one thing I want to talk about. Now it doesn't feel too good to be abandoned especially as a child. First because being that young you really don't have a sense of time. A child thinks that 10 minutes seems like a whole day. When you tell your child that I'll be right back, they say ok or start to cry, either way when you be gone for a long time they feel like you are never coming back. We lived in Chicago, I remember we went to my grandmother's house in the car with this guy. We got to her house, I clearly hear my granny say at the door, you can go but don't take those kids. Her exact words. But my mom left with us anyway. We was taking this long, long ride at night.

I remember seeing these bright lights and these truck stops. We ended up in Grand Rapids, MI. When day break came through we were in this upstairs apartment above where this preacher lived. The place was a glass company off of Division Street. Diagonally was this store called MS Mallays. I use to love to go there with these teenagers that lived around the corner from us. So one morning my mother said she was going to the store to get some bread.

Mind you the store as I'm looking out the window is diagonally to the left of our place. So she went downstairs out the door. Now instead of her going to the left to the store, I see momma going to the right and ain't seen momma since. I was 8 years old, my sister was 7, and the twins were 11 months old. It began to get a little late and no momma.

The preacher who lived downstairs from us happens to come up with a basket full of apples and left telling us to lock the door. After a while all of a sudden there came a knock on the door, it was the police and they were asking where was mommy. They start looking around the whole apartment asking do the twins have any coats. I was so scared that I said no they don't. So they end up finding some sheets in the closet and wrapped the twins in them and off we all go.

I remember the preacher standing by the door as we were crying for our mother as they took us away. Poor momma. I can't ever imagine when she got back to the apartment and seen that her children were gone, if she ever came back. I know that pain was so devastating. We ended up at this place called Child Haven. The people there were so nice. They place me and the sister together in this room with some more children. And I didn't know what they did with the twins.

This all happened in December of 1970. I don't remember how long we were there but I used to ask the people where are my little twin brother and sister. But to no avail got an answer. Now the people took me and the sister under me to this lady's house to visit and to get acquainted with her. What's so weird is her house was on the street facing the apartment which we all were taken from. And that is where we start to reside. But thanks be to God that after 20 years He united us. Me and my siblings.

In our separation, me and the sister under me were adopted together, and the twins were being taken care of together in the city of Muskegon. One thing about the parents who raised us All believed in bringing us up in the church. So life moves on as I kept wondering every night where are my little brother and sister. I can't wait to see them again. As time passed that I had children and I moved over to Muskegon. So one day my children were playing outside and I was talking on the phone to this lady that said as we were talking, look I know your brother and sister. The conversation we had was about some twins that happened to be a boy and girl and by the names of my brother and sister and just happened to be twenty years old and the birthdays happened to be the same date of the twins.

So I'm like this is not a coincidence. And she said wait a minute, I know the lady who has your brother and sister. She gave me the lady's name and told me she was going to call me back. Now this is so ironic that the woman who I was talking to at that time was my children's step grandmother. And she was good friends with the twins adopted mom. I was so excited that I ran next door to my neighbors Cathy's house to call the number she gave me that I forgot I had a phone. So me being all excited went to call the twins mom and as she answered the phone she heard my voice and said Antionette, and tears immediately filled my eyes and she said hold on I'm on my way. I gave her my address.

As they came (the twins and mom) through the door I was so shocked at how they looked so much like my aunt and uncle who lived in Chicago. There was no doubt in my mind that they were my brother and sister. After 20 long years from 1970-1990 I haven't seen my twins. I called my sister in Grand Rapids to let her know about the good news that just had transpired. I had been abandoned of their love that I always had for them. Missing out on growing up with my sister and brother.

Talking about being robbed of Love. But GOD knew and knows what's best for all of us. You see us four (me, my sister, and the twins) are the remnants of what could have really been a not so good situation. So GOD allowed us to be taken from my maternal mom for so many reasons. But that's another story to be told. Me personally wouldn't change it for nothing in the world. In the abandoning I wanted and longed for my maternal mother, I was upset and mad that I hadn't seen her or my twins, at an early age I still forgave my mother because for some reason I understood her sickness that she had. And if she couldn't take care of us at that moment and it was too much on her in her mind, than there was the reason she left us.

Now don't misunderstand me, Nothing in my mind excuses the fact that you should ever leave your children at any given moment, but something clicked in her head that she couldn't deal with which caused her to leave us in that apartment by ourselves. All I know is she said she was going across the street to the store to get some bread and I ain't seen momma since.

Until years later after I was grown with my own children, GOD placed my real mother back in my life where I ended up having to take care of her because of her illness. We talked, argued, laughed, and cried, that I was able to say ok it was like that and that is what happened that I was truly able to forgive. Not saying it was right, but in order for me not to hold any grudges or hate than I had to forgive her and move on. I had to repent to her about some thoughts I had towards her because I was mad she left us. But after we had that talk I was glad and still loved her and most importantly I Forgave her.

For this part of my life (My Purpose Is) was to still love and Forgive. You know something, before we would go to bed, while she was in my care, I would say I love you momma as I would to my children and momma would never say it back to me. She would just say OK but it was alright because as I said we got it together and once you learn a person and know the majority of how they are then you can excuse some of their actions to a degree.

REALITY CHECK

Here I want to make perfectly sure that you understand that this is not to hurt or offend anyone. This is only to have you aware and to those who have experienced and are going through similar if not the same things that I've experienced. I need you to understand that there are different types of things that people experience in this world that hurts them. Thank GOD Almighty that we in today's world haven't experienced the abuse of the Medieval world.

Today there is rape, robbery, shootings, cannibalism, just to name a few. Back in the medieval and barbaric days, you had those that were torn apart from limb to limb, burned at the stakes, eaten alive, stakes driven up their backsides, just to name a few. We cry about the sins of today not paying attention to how Blessed we really are regardless of how we are being treated. Not excusing the wrongs of today because sin is sin of All times no matter which time period people are and were in. There are so, so, many people out there that have lost their way of living and of who they are, turning to drugs, sex, and lies because of the secrets that the devil has fed to them and tricked their minds into thinking that they did something wrong. To the point of the demons they dream about over and over again that lurks in the corner of their minds, have them thinking that if they share their (hidden secrets) with someone that it won't be believed. On the other hand they could have been threatened that if you say anything about what goes on, then you will regret it.

Some demons have it where things seems like it's ok to do, making it seem fun with their luring ways, making like it feels good, that it's just us, don't nobody know, you won't say nothing, I won't say nothing type thing. (Especially As A Child) which leads some to being very curious and trying things that's not for their benefit. But Satan is a lie, liar, and the father of lies. He don't care Nothing about any human being or any type of flesh on this earth, back then and even today. He knows that he has a short time left on this earth and wants to kill everyone.

You see some demons have a way of hiding behind fear. Not the kind of fear that spells out False A Evidence Appearing Real although he does use falsehood about things, but the kind of fear that keeps it a Secret. (THE REALITY OF THINGS.) For a long, long, time I've held things deep inside me that it had me believing this was all my fault. As in I was crazy, I wasn't pretty, not light skinned enough, my hair was too short, I'm not smart enough, look how black I was, I was even given a nickname called monkey which had me feeling mighty low and ugly. Just to name a few.

These were things that were repeatedly said to me that I even had my children looking at me in the mirror talking about ahuh yes I do look see. Had me feeling for years that didn't nobody love me or like me. For one thing I have to remember that I was put on this earth to be loved in the right way and not for anyone to like me but for me to help someone else save themselves from the mean things I've experienced and from this untoward generation of evil that they encounter somewhere in their life. (My Purpose Is) to let you know (You Can Overcome and You Will Win) because that's your purpose. Evil doesn't love you.

I've let time and people blame me for things that I never even had control of. I'm wondering what did I do wrong and why this or that is happening to me, couldn't wait until things got better. When in reality I was very, very intelligent because of the things that surrounded me at an early age, kept me enlighten about a Lot Of Things that I probably shouldn't even have known about as a child. I remember my mom telling me to (speak up butt mouth gone visiting) which means Talk when she or other people would talk to me but I would just sit there listening and soaking up all the things that were being said.

This is also one of the ways that a person with positive dreams and hopes never bring their beauty, their dreams, and goals to life because they have been robbed. Robbed of time and their inner mind which kept them captivated with whatever it was that held their attention at the time, if that makes sense.

Rather if it was the things they experienced physically or the knowledge of things that they weren't able to express. And when I would try to speak and express A myself, others would say, aww go somewhere with that as if I didn't know what I was talking about, or look at me like I was nuts. Only to find out later that oooh my God that did happened to her and ok you were right. And also I was so afraid to come forth with anything because of the shame, the embarrassment, the rejection, the hurt, the low self-esteem, feeling lonely and grew up thinking that oh well I ain't never been nothing anyway so may as well keep being the way I was made into, which led me down the dark street life of drugs and crime to try to escape the pain inside. So don't be ashamed to come forth because you have a story to share as well.

I Thank the Almighty GOD above for delivering me out of that dark ugly mold which seemed to have had no end into a beautiful way of loving myself and living the light of life. We will talk about that later. But, once again, The devil Is A Lie Amen. If I may interject something here that I said I'd never tell. But in order to help someone and let them know that you were and are not alone, then I'm going to share. But first I will say that I have Forgiven those and still ask to be forgiven by those that I yet have to come into contact with. AGAIN, this is not to hurt or downgrade or put anyone on front street.

This is for those that are still ashamed to come forth with the truth about themselves of what they did against their bodies and allowed themselves to go through and what others did to them so they can be set free from the enemies hand and be free in their minds and spirits to move on with their lives. Amen. I have held this in for so many years and even though it hurts when I think to myself from time to time, I'm ok with it now and have finally come to peace with these situations that I can Now tell my story of how I Bounced Back for My Purpose Is.

I'm telling this now because I was tired of holding it in for too long of a time. I was stagnated. I used to say to my girls all the time that I never was a virgin. I would say it in a jokingly way because I really didn't know how to talk about my pain, especially about the hurt coming from family members. I said this because I can truly remember from the time I was three to four years an old that this person used to feel on me in a molesting way. You know between my legs in my private area used to hurt.

I used to have nightmares even as an adult about this long hallway, where I would have to stoop down and get on my knees, being pushed from behind to get to the room that was way in the back. Well once I reached the room, there used to be these ugly looking monsters that used to be all over me. Hurting me really bad. Those dreams were actually my reality when I was a child. It was so weird that when I turned 54 years old visiting my cousin in Chicago, that as we were reminiscing about the good times, that as we continue talking, that he was describing the basement to me. No it wasn't my cousin who molested me.

I looked at him in disbelief because there is no way that he knew my nightmarish dreams. I start crying because he didn't know and I for sure never shared it with nobody back then because I didn't have any inclination why was this person doing this to me or how do I go about saying something to someone. But know that GOD Always has himself a witness. Not long ago in 2007 I was talking with my biological mother sharing with her about different things in my life and what had happened to me, that she said to me yeah she found out later in her life what was happening to me. This happened for years. Now for some reason I have always been afraid to go into my granny basement, and that's the reason. I remember when my birth mother would get me and my sister ready to go to granny house, this was before the twins were born, as we arrived, I would be scared of the downstairs. I have to get this out because as long as I keep this in, I never want to be around this person.

Freedom of the mind is a great key to living without grudges or hatred. What the saying is that confession is good for the soul. I was so messed up in my head that as I got a little older and needed a bill paid or something that I said I'll get some money from this person since he wants to act like that. Just sickening. Oh don't look at me like that as you read this with your sanctimonious self because let your truths be told okay so we all can be helpers one to another. Acting like a trick or something was that time of day. I was really screwed all the way up in my head till I was hating this person. But Thank GOD for Salvation. And talk about a curse. And I couldn't afford to hate people so I'll just exposed that demonic spirit. As I mentioned before that I have to forgive in order for me to be forgiven and set free. You cannot grow into spiritual maturity and move forward with your life if you have these different types of hurts and animosities in your heart.

This had an effect on me in several ways to the point of I didn't like boys or men and didn't want nobody touching me. And as a child coming up, I was always wondering about the body and being promiscuous in my mind, as being a little freak, but you couldn't touch me. It was nasty. Boy! Talking about that Mind. I had to be delivered. I later found out that a man and woman are supposed to be together and love each other in order for the world to go around. There is a natural way of doing so, not by incest or any other way, example, rape.

People are supposed to be in love with each other and have children as GOD had planned from the beginning. Now after I ran away in 1998 from my adopted mom to my granny house in Chicago I felt free until I was again confronted with that basement, but I was ok because my aunt was staying down there and it was really pretty and positive unlike back in the day where it was dark, cold and haunting.

Plus I met this guy who I later found out was the leader of a gang set on the west side that had me preoccupied with things. I was sixteen years old. Young People please be careful not to grow up before your time because you might not like the situation that you find yourself in. Everything and everybody that presents themselves to you are not always glitter and gold. This is one of those things that it looked good, I tricked you, now I got you, and now you're thinking to yourself, how can I escape. It's all fun in the beginning but not good in the in between or the end. I did however got something beautiful out this ordeal and that was a beautiful baby girl. But let me share with you a tiny bit before she was born in 1980. I need you to understand and read me real good.

Understand that it is never ok to accept abuse. Rather if it's verbal, mental, physically, or whatever kind of abuse, just know that it is never ok. Know your worth of who you are and what you won't or will stand for. Talking from experience, a lot of times we take it just to hold on to a person cause they say they love you. Not realizing that you are putting the abuser in a bad mental state as well. They probably don't want to be that way but because you are letting it happen gives them the power over you and they think that you like it and it's ok for them to treat you that way. They beat on you and then turn right around and tell you, see what you made me do. You know I love you. NOT. And then want to make love to you. Not so.

As they continue with these different

abuses, it gets worse each and every time. And you stay there and keep letting them come back or whatever the case may be, it won't be stopped until you really gets fed up, and by that time it's too late because what will end up happening is one or the other will be in the hospital or jail or even dead. Stop taking this type of abuse and stand up for yourself. Know your worth. Rather you believe it or not, you are even abusing that abuser by allowing this to happen.

People you have to stop telling yourself out of fear that it's my fault. Talking about If I wouldn't did this or said that then he wouldn't beat me. I do love him and he really loves me, no. I don't care, it's Not Your Fault. Oh yeah, men get abused too. Even a child knows to keep their hands to themselves. Even a child knows when they start talking real good that that wasn't a nice thing to say or do to someone. You can tell they know, just look at the expressions on their little faces.

So don't you dare say uuuh I didn't know better, that spirit is of the devil. Even this, you might have been abused as a child and think that it's ok because mom and dad said this to you while you got whooped, they say I'm beating you because I love you. So again you think that it's fine. It will and can spill over into your adulthood believing that if I don't get beat than that person doesn't love you.

The devil is a lie. And this is also where we get these adult abusers from, doing things to other people because they think it's ok and really haven't had the psychological help as a child to help them rightly divide what's good and healthy with your grown self. Ooooh Jesus help my thoughts right now Lord lol. Naw y'all know I love y'all. It was even in my mind that one day you are going to get yours. But how many of you know that Vengeance is mine saith the LORD. And guess what, I forgave. And thank GOD that I didn't take matters into my own hands which I had the chance to but things didn't turn out good for the people who did this to me.

Parents, yeah we know that children have a wild imagination and will lie because of the make believe world that they want to live in, But when that child comes to you about any kind of abuse I mean Any kind of abuse, You listen to them and listen good because in the end we all need the right kind of love. LORD please have mercy on my soul and their souls even as I write this. (My Purpose Is) to let you beautiful people know to know your worth and you don't have to live with any kind of abuse that will and can lead you to suicide. It's Not worth it. Live and stay alive until you're called to Christ.

BARGAIN

Ok I really have to get this off my chest. Now I as I do this you will notice that some of what I say will be direct and straight to the point. So please try not to be like, "O I thought she was so saved. I am but this is to help someone be honest with themselves and let them know it's ok go ahead and do this. I have been so focused on the wrong things all these years that I am so far behind time as this lady Evangelist Rochelle Lee once told me.

For years as I have been in this way of the Apostolic Faith, I know that I have been rooted and grounded in the word of GOD, you know fasting and praying the 30 days right after I got baptized and being filled with the Holy Ghost. I was on the roll all the time with the fasting because it felt like that everytime I did that it felt so good like something was running through my hair and I had noticed that my hair had begun to get grey like right in the front you know a nice patch it was so pretty. And when I did these fasts I noticed that when I pray for whatever that thing would come to past.

For one thing I stuck to one of my favorite scriptures and that's Matthew 6:33 which states But seek ye First the kingdom of GOD and His righteousness; and all these things shall be added unto you. And I'm telling you that I used to go wild about the benefits that was being reaped because I loved to do that {seek Him First} and I didn't have not any problems getting whatever I wanted because He was already taking care of my needs.

See I wouldn't fast for cars, houses, shoes, or anything material, but I would ask Him for spiritual things like wisdom and spiritual strength and Always saying Lord GOD bless others. On top of that I would put this scripture into action, the one that states Those who lack Wisdom, let them ask of GOD who giveth to all men liberally, and upbraideth not, and it shall be given him. James 1:5. The more I fasted and set up under the teaching of the Word of GOD I begin to get stronger and stronger and remembering things from my past that sort of kind of had a negative connotation to it I would Pound it into my Children that don't you let nobody and I mean nobody tell you that you can't do whatever you want to do because I'm a witness yes you can.

I remember being told in private in a lot of instances that I would never be nothing, that no man is gone ever want me and that I would have a house full of nasty kids. But how many know that you don't have to be what you were told or not. That's why I used to beat the mess out of my kids when they bedrooms and my house would be messed up when I got home from work or whatnot. Now wait when my babies was just kids I Loved to get my kids cleaned up, get their food cooked and feed them and after that I would smoke my joint and watch soap operas. This was before the Holy Ghost y'all.

In the night I would repeat the process but at night I have my cigarette and grab my

Bible and dig deep reading it getting excited looking up asking GOD certain things and soaking up what I just read. But yeah I was instilling into them that yes ain't nobody have no business in your bedroom but dog gone it your bathroom and kitchen should always be clean. And as they grew I know that they saw what I was talking about. Because for one they was experiencing and reaping benefits of me telling them that and pushing the FAITH into them. That if you say it and pray it believe it and it be GOD will that you can have my Loves.

Secondly, I see results of how they do with my grandchildren and they would say Momma I see what you mean Now. But anyway, I know now that it was knowledge from GOD that I was experiencing with that feeling and I just wanted more and more and more. Because what as they say Knowledge is what, Power. Now I wouldn't let that get to me because I use to say Lord whatever I get please don't let me get the big head about it otherwise take it. Now I don't believe that He would take His knowledge away from you but other things yes He would allow the enemy to take from you if you don't have your priorities right as far as He's concern amen. So with that being said, I guess I can use an example right here.

My children's father was already over here in Muskegon and said why don't me and the children just move over here. Now I was already fearful because it seems like every time on the news you would hear that some woman and her kids got burned up in her house. Somebody just got killed in the projects. You know something always was going on in Muskegon. But I remember I said Lord you get me over here safely to Muskegon I will serve you. We're talking about making a bargain. Now that's what I said ok.

Now He kept His end of the bargain just by doing just that. I get over here and He start blessing me from staying with the children's aunt GOD rest her soul, to me saying to my children's dad that you have to get us a house. He did. He got up and went to talk to this man and I had to meet with him and guess what yes we got blessed with the man's mother's house which was fully furnished with two grapevines on one side of the house and gardening on the other. Talking about the goodness of Jesus before I even knew who He was. So I got in there and GOD start blessing where I got a nursing job, a house full of my kind of furniture, on top of the furniture that was already there, a car, classes at the college, and you know the works.

There was a church right next door to us and I went there 1 time. Went to another church probably 2 times. Oh I was still into my bible cause that's what I loved to do But something was wrong with this picture because Imma tell you something don't you ever try to bargain with the Lord because you can't. First my children's dad left me by being incarcerated, things started being repossessed, lost my job and things just for some reason started to go bad for me.

Woooow really all because I made a bargain and didn't keep it by not serving Him like I promised.

The church was right next door, I wasn't doing nothing on Sunday's where I couldn't attend. I mean I didn't have to work on Sunday's, I didn't have class, my homework was already done because I only had two classes because I didn't want to overload myself because I did have my children to take care of. Um let me just say something here to encourage some young mother with a child or children. It really is not hard at all raising children if you love and your mind is made up. If you know for a fact that you have to eat, bathe, need to be groomed and loved, then so does your child. So I was free to worship but I didn't keep my promise. Think what you want to, that has a really, really, big part of it and plays a big part of your life. Try it and find out.

Now back to where I want to talk about yes. Oh yeah, when and after I got sanctified yes it was so good. But I noticed that I had a zeal that I just wanted to do this and that for GOD that I used to ask questions and I was told to go to the 66 books of the bible and I would be like huh, but would do just that and that's how I end up with the Bachelor's Degree graduated Magna Cum Laude thanks be to GOD. I remember not hearing correctly that who all wants to sign up and by that I wasn't paying too much attention because I thought it was just another bible class but it end up being bible school.

Ok now you know how they use to give praise for this and appreciate that, well I say I wanted a pat on the back too. Let me say something right here, Never Ever look for praise from people. I was as they say, a babe in the Lord and learned the hard way even though I knew I always loved GOD. Yes I use to lead these songs and the saints use to come up to me and be like you sung that song. Ok don't get me wrong I love to sing but I'm talking about things on another Plato. I guess what I'm really trying to say is I wanted a pat too and some praise too ya know what I mean. It just seemed to me I would never hear my name being called out loud. You know call my name out. The only time it seems that would happen is when we would have visiting churches come and the Spirit would be so high and then one of the Bishops or Elders or one of the big people would look around the crowd and me with my big eyes would just be looking around hoping and praying that GOD would just say something to them and let them know that I want to get closer to Him, and to see if they knew something in my life that I needed them to say.

By we all having the same spirit that's not divided they should feel what I feel and know what I'm almost thinking right. And by GOD Almighty it would happen. They would call me and read my spirit and honestly it would be what I just asked Him or needed. Come on now no it wasn't no witch craft but a selfsame spirit. But they would leave and I would still look for that calling on my life. You nut GOD just gave it to you but evidently you somewhere in your finite mind still looking for a pat. Go on somewhere girl with that because GOD is the only one who gets Glory like that and who deserves that Plato of pats sort to speak amen. GOD steady telling you through your pastor and others your call but you ain't hearing Him. He was telling you Face to Face in His Word.

What I was looking for was right in my face all the time. He gave me Proverbs the 4th Chapter to begin with when I first got sanctified. Let me tell you how because first of all and foremost Your Gift Will Make Room For You. Proverbs 18;16 states A man's gift maketh room for him, and bringeth him before great men. See I was looking for something that was there all along. But anyway, traveling with the singing group that I was a part of. Teaching in school, being a secretary for twenty-six different churches, driving the church bus. And that's just to name a few. So I didn't have any business trying to get no recognition from nobody because GOD Already was setting me before people, great and small.

Y'all do know that I'm kicking myself in the butt right now because I know He just revealed this to me as I'm writing this. He is so Awesome. Stop looking for praise from man. Stop trying to make bargains. If you want to be seen by men so bad, well that's your reward and it won't last or be remembered. But wait I just want to be heard. Ok you don't have to be a preacher which I kept saying to myself that's what I want to do, you don't have to be in front of a lot of people to preach to someone.

My God what do you think Teaching Is huh, you have to stand before people to do that, or it can be as simple as one on one, so stop asking. Oh praise break right here I Love You Lord. You know even my kids were even in this Zion Bible Institution. They had begun to prosper in the Word also. As I used to clean the church and the upper room I would tell my children by the time I get home I want a summary of what you have read. You know just a chapter or two. I would have them fasting and praying too. I even put my fishes and cat on a fast too. At that time I meant heaven. I still do. They use to go on all kinds of trips with the church as I had to stay home and work. Getting all kinds of good grades at school, starting choirs at the school that haven't had one since 1960something and getting all types of Certificates and things themselves. I mean being put in front of the crowds before people.

So I have to say this because all this is coming from a person who was told in secret that I will never be nothing or have nothing. But can we say But GOD. Um please don't Misunderstand me, that person raised me and made me into the very person I am today. And I Love that person to life itself. Because she also taught me structure and gave me stability in my life when I had nobody else. Taught me to cook, clean, garden even though I don't garden, morals, and mostly about the Almighty Creator.

You know as I got grown and had my own family, I asked why was I treated the way I was and she told me because she expected more from me and out of me. Because let's be honest I was an obedient child yes but there was some rebellion going on too as far as my schooling at that time. My focus was never on school as it could have been because it was always on my birth mother, like where are you and why did you leave me. So that's why I used to get my butt tore up.

Momma, the one who raised me, didn't play that ignorant stuff ok. And that's where I said Can't nobody tell me it's hard raising children and that you can't do it. Oh yes you Can. If you yourself when getting up have to go to the bathroom, get cleaned up, needs to eat, need love and comfort, then so does your child. Take that negative and turn it into positive baby. And I do thank you momma. If you say to me that I can't, I be like don't say that to me because I can. I say this that the only thing can't is GOD can't lie. Because He's not a man that He should lie nor son of man that He has to repent. If He said it He's gone do it and when He do it, He's gone make it good. Paraphrasing. Numbers 23:19. And that is how I feel, don't tell me I can't cause that would push me even harder. Not that I had to prove anything to anybody but I had to first prove it to myself. I'm talking in instances like raising my children, getting jobs and accomplishing things. But you still can't bargain with GOD, you will not win if you start getting the big head about this and that because of pride getting in the way. You will come up short. Remember that whenever you try to promise or bargain with the LORD. I did eventually got it together.

That's how I was able to accomplish the spiritual things and He blessed me with the things I mentioned above.

MY FIRST HEALING

I want to talk a little bit about the time while I was saved in the Holy Ghost that I was so, so, on fire for the Lord that I had went through so much with my body that I said I wished I never asked the question of, how can a person backslide or why so much pain? That is 1 of the questions that I believe you should never ask. Let me just say when you are on a journey for GOD there is no question that when you are called to do a work that your gift or gifts will make room for you.

You come into the newness of life you have a zeal that nobody in the world can take from you. You know GOD was the one who gave you this new way of living. You know that it was the Lord who saved you. You don't want to hurt nobody not even an ant. You treat everybody with the most warmth of love that you have. You want everybody to walk in this newness of life with you. You are always fasting and praying for yourself and everybody that you can think of and or come into contact with. You will become the pastor and first lady helper depending if you're a brother or sister. You attend all the saints meetings in which instructions are without question as in if you send me yes I will go. You learn your word always studying from front and back. You join all the auxiliaries there are. Not to mention last but not least that your tithes and offerings are also without question.

Now this is for the ones who really and truthfully are in love with the Lord. So I say for me that I should have probably never asked that question, how can you backslide and why does a person go through so much trouble and pain after experiencing all the goodness that you've tasted of the Lord. I use to say all the time, how can I tell somebody about what GOD can do if I never experience anything so that I can be that witness. Well I will tell you how it turned out for me. You look at the clergymen with such awww that you want to become just like them. Not really knowing anything about how they got in that position nor the suffering it took for them as they became that person who they are. Not saying that they're not qualified because they are otherwise GOD would not have called them. But only if you really knew you probably would have been like Jesus, father take this cup from me.

Now as I was doing all this studying with fasting and praying I felt that I was so strong that couldn't nothing touch me. At that time in my life, it really couldn't to be honest. For instant after I got into it like I was, I stopped taking my children to the doctor. Just being honest here. When they would get sick I would take the oil that I had got blessed and would put it on them in a minute and wait for their healing. And it would work. If their grades would become a little low I would pray and anoint them and believe me that their grades would pull up. I would get a bad headache and lay hands on myself and yes that thing would leave in Jesus Name.

I would pray mostly for wisdom and I got it. I would touch a house and or cars and would get it. Everything that I would pray for and about, that thing would come to pass. But something happened along the way. Oh wait I was always busy cleaning the church, going to school, going to work, and taking care of my children and home. But something happened.

As long as I was busy I know for a guaranteed fact that I was in good health. Well there was a time in my life that I was preparing for a husband without really paying attention again to what was taking place. When I would wash me and my children clothes that I would pretend to wash my husband's clothes although there was no man there. When I would cook and set my children down to eat I would also set a plate down for my husband which was not there yet. I would do different things that would involve a husband who was not yet there. Oh I fell to mention that I drove the church bus also to and from the church.

I stayed busy which moving around as I did help kept my body functioning right along with the right foods that I ate at the time. Now at that time I wasn't looking for no man but my private actions in my home was otherwise. As I drove the bus I knew everyone that I picked up and dropped off because I would go according to their addresses. To show you how God had the children of Israel blinded to some things, I can attest to it somewhat because as I would pick up people knowing them all, I never seen this one guy who would get on the bus. I was picking him up along with his mother at the same with dropping him off with her.

One Wednesday night as I picked up for bible class when it was over my then pastor came to me and said Sister there is a brother here who would like to take you out to dinner and I said he can take you. I was so shocked that I said you told him yeah. I was a little bit upset because I wasn't looking for na man. But yet acting out as if there was a man around lol. And that was really the first time I saw him. So ok after I dropped the people off he and I went out. And that was the beginning of the courtship between us. Time moved on to the point of he didn't want me to do anything especially cleaning the church. He felt it was a man's job to do. But I loved my work because I was doing it unto the Lord. But he wasn't having that.

The more we got involved with each other the more my work became slack. He would cook, clean the church, and drive the bus. I felt like I couldn't do anything. And this was the beginning of my body slowing down. The only thing I was allowed to do was wash clothes and keep the children and house clean. I wasn't use to not doing my church cleaning and bus driving. But in doing so as I said my body begin to slow down. I remember me in secret wanting to bless him with a child. I go to the doctor to make sure everything was fine.

Well a week later the doctor called me on the phone and said that they need me to come back in to discuss some things. Me not thinking anything and being excited, when I get there they tell me that they found a bunch of abnormalities in a certain area and need to do this thing called a biopsy. They set the appointment up for me to return. When I went back they told me that I have cancer cells that needed immediate attention. I had to keep going back and forth to the doctor.

See as your body starts to settle down things begin to happen and wake up that was dormant all your life. They begin to show their ugly face. As long as you're moving around you're good. I didn't tell nobody but like a few people. I didn't know much about this cancer business. They gave me medicines to take that made me so sick to my stomach. I passed out a few times. I became real sick. But you know what by me still being headstrong in the bible, I happened to be at bible class one Wednesday night listening to the lesson, which happens to be about the ten lepers.

There were ten guys who had leprosy

and they all got healed but only one came back to show himself to the priest and to say thank you. Well that was me. I said now Lord you already told me in your word that you would not put none of these diseases on me as you did the Egyptians. I wasn't going to accept that something was wrong with me. I heard that lesson and ran with it. As a little time went by I returned to the doctor for further results and they told me as I remember that the cancer was gone. Thanking GOD that it wasn't in these stages of no return. You say what you'll be and have. Believing that I was going to be healed, I was for My Purpose Is.

FALL FROM GRACE

The enemy don't and didn't want me to tell this but I have to let others know it's OK to tell the truth to get help and help others. It's never too late to tell the truth as long as the Almighty GOD allows you to get up one more day. I would like to let you know about the time I fell short from Grace.

It started when my car crashed with me in it off the highway by the exit of Nunica, MI. I was on my way to work at the University in Allendale. I was doing 50 miles an hour on the highway in the left lane. I was just saying yes Lord and praying I'm ready to do your will GOD. The radio station normally wouldn't play gospel music doing third shift hours. All the times I would turn the radio on while going to work I've never heard the gospel being played.

I heard a church song come on and got real excited. This was doing the month of April of 1998. So I was adjusting my seat belt when all of a sudden my car turned over and over off the highway and all I remember is me crying Jesus, Jesus. The devil tried to kill me because I said at that time yes I'm ready Lord. I'm talking about yes I was really ready to do His will. I had already been rooted and grounded in His word eight years strong at that time, but wanted more from Him as in spreading the Good News of Jesus to others.

Not saying I wasn't witnessing because I was already doing that and bringing people to Him. But something more was what I wanted. As the car was turning over I know what I saw and that was something really, really tall. I couldn't see a face but as I believe it was Jesus or an ministering angel. And I believe it was him who set the car facing upward toward the highway so somebody could see the lights of the car. All I know is a guy in a semi-truck and a station wagon with a couple in it who came down and helped me out the car. The couple was the one who took me back to Muskegon. They dropped me off at my then Pastor and

First Lady's house.

I never got a chance to thank them, but would send a prayer up for them saying Lord bless them. I couldn't believe what just happened that I didn't go to the hospital that night. All I wanted was some prayer. So when I got home to my family, they were all in shock when I told them what happened. I remember I kept telling the children to pinch me or something so I can know that I'm still alive.

As the weeks went by I was still able to get to the University with a co-worker but after some weeks I started to really feel bad all over my body. I did eventually go to the doctor and they still were able to detect the points of my body that was messed up. They did give me a lot of medicine to take but for some reason it seems that I needed something stronger. See in those days I didn't believe in taking medicine so I would lay hands on myself. But the pain and my Faith were at war with each other. Me not paying attention that I was still in the fleshly body. So by my husband already was doing things that I have heard about in the streets, I asked him to get some stuff for me so he can put it on my back to sooth the pain. But instead of putting it on my back, that is when I was introduced to how to smoke it.

Like really what was I thinking about rubbing it on me anyway, I didn't know about that drug like that. I was still sanctified in the church. So as I was being showed how to smoke I was getting yelled at because I didn't know what I was doing. So when I got the hang of it that night of trying it, it hit me so hard till I said ok, ok I like this and honestly I didn't feel any pain at the time. The trick of the devil. Always be on guard for he knows what to introduce to you to really knock you off your feet and faith with GOD and to get you back into the world when you are going through something.

Now this wasn't an everyday and no everynight thing because I was still going to church which end up being the beginning of my backsliding state of mind. But GOD will keep your mind even in the midst of your wrong doing. When things started to get a little out of hand that I wanted to stop, I went to my pastor and told him the truth about what I was doing and I asked him, I said Bishop but I want to know why is it now when I tried to smoke that I can't get high. And why when I do wrong it seems like I was still getting blessings. I mean real blessings. I will never forget what he said to me and that is GOD has something in store for you.

I wasn't understanding at that time what he meant that GOD has something in store for me. And bishop said that GOD loves you dearly. That's what he said to me. I started to cry like a baby. He is a Merciful GOD. One thing about it before I would do the wrong, I would always say, Now Lord you know what I'm gone do before I do it because you the one who made me, now Please Keep My Mind. And even today as I write this letter to you the reader, I know for a guaranteed fact that Jesus will protect your mind. I could have lost my mind, I could have gone crazy or anything, but GOD for My Purpose Is. Hallelujah.

There happens to be another time where I fell into the drugs again and wanted so desperately to leave that stuff alone. The enemy knows also that you are somebody special to GOD and that you have a Purpose to fulfill especially if you profess that you belong to the Almighty. When I tell you that you can have what you want especially when you get to thinking about your children, your surroundings, your character, and all, you will fight for your freedom. I had too much to lose.

Once again I start to cry out to GOD where I start telling myself that Greater Is He that's in me than he that's in the world. Talking to myself in the mirror that I can't die like this. Rebuking that dope demon that had me captivated to a degree, I said get your stinking self away from me. So I started to do things that were positive so I wouldn't let those smoke thoughts get to me. The reason why I would think about it though was the place where I resided which was at the hotel with my girls, and the school where I was teaching had closed down, at that time my car was broken down, just to name a few. I tried to go to church but it seemed so fake to me and ritualistic that I didn't want to attend.

Nothing personal against the pastor and wife because they were and still are some beautiful people of the Most High. I still love them. One thing about drugs it will have you blaming other people for you mess up. It's everybody else's fault that you're not about your business. Especially when you see everybody around you prospering, smiling, and seems to be in good health. Well if you stop giving your money to the dope man you can have these things too. I'm not about materials but life itself, instead of feeling like you done lost your dog.

It was my fault. I'm just being honest. I wanted to go back home to Muskegon to start all over again. And GOD allowed me that escape after me praying for Him to deliver me. Now I want to know what's so special about little ole Net. The reason I say this is because when I asked to be delivered first I use to say (anytime Lord) and He did. I would say this everyday and every time I think about it, I would say Any Time Lord deliver me Please. I made it up in my mind that enough is enough. Here is the thing.

Some people are so far out there that it seems no hope for them, that they have lost their will even to live. Thinking even suicidal thoughts because they want out so much. They try to stop on their own, tried even being around other positive people to keep their minds off of it, they tried to even go to Narcotic Anonymous Classes, tried to go the Rehabs Centers but none of those things seem to work or stick. And that's because you have to want it for yourself. One reason it doesn't stick is because it's what they family wants for them. But you have to want it for yourself. Yes your family wants to see you free from that because who just want to see their love ones in that state of mind or even die. Nobody ok. Yea the addict might want it for themselves but has really lost their will. People plays a really big part in this. Listening to people talk about them, criticizing them, acting like they are better than them like they don't have skeletons in their closets. Acting like they never did nothing against their bodies.

Well I have big news for you, when you were born you were not perfect. So yeah, back to me. Acting and pretending that oh it's just recreational for me but no I was in a real bad state. I thank the good LORD that He is a GOD that has everlasting Mercies. I've always kept myself clean in my addiction because I have this saying that You don't have to look like what you do. People use to say to me that they respected me because I wasn't out there like that. But in fact yes I was. Not that I ever, ever heard anybody talking about me, I still was an addict. You know the ones that they call closet smoker. Well I said again, that everything ain't everybody's business.

My children, the two youngest and my son were the biggest witnesses that were around to see how I was in my state. The few times that I feel my children knew when I was high was I would always pass out my money to them lol. They didn't go without for real. No I never prostituted myself, I never shoplift to get high, I never sold my stuff out of my house, or stole from people to get high but I still was in a bad, bad way that needed immediate attention. Because if I would have died, straight to hell I believe I was going for living the life with the devil. So again why me.

He, GOD loved and loves me and that He is not of respective of person. Jesus went to the cross for this very type of thing. Only when I recognized it, admitted it, and asked for forgiveness by going to the church building which is the hospital for the helpless seeking help, then that's when I became free. I not once had to attend NA,

AA, any facility, classes, or anything of the nature to be delivered off that drug. I meant in my heart and the intent of my heart that I wanted to be free. It wasn't because if I go to those places I'm gone be ashamed although I was ashamed of my own self. That really was not the case. I said It's a Mind Thing. I said no, not me, no more, now come see about me LORD.

He did just that and put me back into position with Him and to Him I will owe GOD the rest of my life. If I go into someone's home or any place on this earth and it even seems like I smell that drug, I cringes. I can't stand it. I dare not to even think about it because I might die should I go back to that drug again and I refuse to die like that. How many know that every time you try to and do right that stinkin thinkin evil would be hanging around. Yes when I first got delivered the enemy would try me by saying do I want to go smoke I would get offended and cuss, oh yeah the devil is a lie. That's his job for a person to be robbed of their life especially if you have a purpose. You can't tell me that I can't be free from that slave mentality of anything that tries to alter my state of mind because I will be free. My will was for me to be free. (My Purpose Is). And I know for a fact that I've been delivered. I said it, I asked for it, and it happened.

There is a saying that a lot of people flow with and that is The Mind Is A Terrible Thing To Waste. Yes I understand why they say terrible. I say that the mind is a Beautiful place that holds the best of all thinking, and that is Knowledge. I say it like this that The Mind is a huge bowl that holds beautiful things that expresses the both sides of feelings that comes to thought. It's up to you to how you're going to use it. If I say within my mind that I will conquer these things that comes up against me, then I think that this is a beautiful way of thinking and put it to action it will come to pass. But if you sit there and let the thoughts of your mind dictate to you making negative actions then that's where you go wrong. Be careful how you fulfill your thoughts because the Mind Is Beautiful and Awesome. Even in creating evil, the mind is still so awesome. So with this mindset of mine, I will think on the things that are positive and that will keep my mind in perfect peace. And again that's how I got delivered for (My Purpose Is).

SOUTH BEND

The reason why I want to share this short story with you is because when you fall into sin like I have, you can't blame nobody else but yourself and you have to recognize the particular spirit that's dealing with your soul that's trying to control you and send you to the place of torment and fire. So with that being said, I just want to talk about how GOD freed me from this experience while I was in the wrong way.

It was actually the time when I was in South Bend, Indiana after I ran away from problems at home in Muskegon, and I was teaching at the school things had got a little hectic there for me. My first husband had moved to South Bend and he was staying at the hotel out there. Me and my girls we were already in my apartment and my son of course. But yeah I was teaching at the school and having a lot of complications with a few of the teachers there you know. Not realizing that it was just another test of my faith. Oh I loved my job but I had to deal with the spirit of whoredom and aggravation. Me loving my job had nothing to do with it.

I was being transferred from the school to the porter building you know from the big building to the porter building, that was the problem because I loved and was well set with the students I already had. So that set me back because I started not to care being in the porter building was for me was very depressing. No room to move around in, because they had three or four other classes within one unit. So I would start getting high before I went to work because I wanted out.

So how that start working out for me was my car start acting crazy, I start complaining about how my back was hurting from the car accident I had earlier and a fall on ice I taken as well at the university, sitting in an uncomfortable position seeing I didn't have a desk anymore. I just wanted out. oh wait, wait, wait let me backup, first of all the apartment that I was leasing at the time was up for me to renew it, and they weren't going to renew the lease because the expiration date had passed for me to turn a new application in at that time.

I didn't really want to stay there anymore either because it was too much gangster stuff going around in that area and that's how we end up staying out there at the hotel with my husband. So me and my girls as we stayed out there with my husband turned out to be an unpleasant stay. Please don't misunderstand me, he wasn't a bad person but just had to work on self as we all have to do. Myself included.

Now we both had our own hotel room. His was on the other side of the hotel. But the thing is he would try to come to my room to get high, and come to find out while I would be in the bathroom he was doing things in front of my girls that should not have been done even while I'm there taking my turn in the bathroom. I would close the door because I didn't let them see what I was doing. I have this moto that everything ain't everybody's business. But if you see your child going down that path, then you let them know that that is not the way to go. But until then, yes they knew it because I had already set them down and told them just in case something was to happen to me, but they didn't see me doing it. As we would talk about things from time to time, they would say that they have never seen me do it.

So my middle child end up going to stay with a sister from the church. Okay now it was so much going on I just want to get to the point about how God had delivered me from that drug infested vicinity that I was in at that particular moment. My daughter had ended up going to the juvenile center in which I almost broke down standing in the doorway of the hotel. I didn't break down then but after a few days that reality set in that she really wasn't in my presence I was going nuts and the drugs got a little worse. It was almost 30 days that I hadn't seen her I was beating myself up about it. I couldn't see my daughter and it was my fault. But my youngest baby girl was still with me going through my troubles with me. She was still going to school and all and this is kinda hard for me to talk about because I said I would never leave my kids, wasn't nobody gonna ever have my kids, they would never leave my side and I end up some kind of way not paying attention to my surroundings that my daughter end up being in the juvenile center.

My heart hurt right now but that part is over so I'm fine. We talked about it so it's ok. But anyway, I just want to tell you how I was allowed to be set free from this place one night. One night I was getting real cool in the bathroom while my girls was going to church or they was going somewhere so they wasn't there. It was just me and my husband but anyway I was just in the bathroom getting cool to myself and I set up off the toilet and I looked in the mirror and I had both of my hands on the sides of the sink looking into the mirror, I just start calling out to God because I wanted to be delivered so bad from that dope spirit and as I was rebuking the devil it seemed like that my face was getting so ugly and so distorted. That's how I knew that I was possessed with a type of spirit that it was not of God. You do know that when you backslide from His Spirit that you really do gain seven more unclean spirits and they are nothing nice. So while I was rebuking the devil and everything, my face was continuing getting uglier and uglier that it just did not look like me. It was getting so distorted I was scaring myself.

My hands were clutching the sink so tight as I was fighting this demon. At the same time I was looking into those eyes that was looking into that mirror and the devil eyes looking back at me I begin telling them things, you will release this child of God because she don't belong to you in the name of Jesus. I need you right now even in the name of Jesus you are going to lose this child and let her go. She don't belong to you. You can't have her. Satan you have no power over her. I begin to say repeatedly that greater is He (talking about GOD) that is in me, than he that's in the world. I was just so messed up in the head I start throwing the paraphernalia away and getting cleaned up. I never liked no messy high to begin with. I was just crying and crying and crying out to God and he came through for me because it was like the next day when some of the people came with some stuff to get high with, that I immediately got frustrated at the devil, like leave me alone. I rebuke you Satan.

I went to the owner and begged for some money so I can go back home to Muskegon. I could have said come on in and got as high as I wanted to but I was running for my life. He gave me the money, I loaded up my car and girls and left real quick. The owner told me don't come back like this and I promised him that I never will. I haven't been back since but one time and that was to thank the owner years later. Now some reading this might say to themselves, man it seems like she had been getting free from the drug life so many times. Well how many know that three times you're out? Ok, so I went through this crisis three different times and I said that the third time I'm Out as in Never return to it again. Especially now that I'm really back in GOD having a few death scares, and waiting on His return being afraid that I will burn in hell if I miss His coming, I'm Out.

My Purpose Is to let you know that I don't care how many times you fall because of your circumstances, Please I beg of you Repent and to call continuously on GOD with the intentions of making your life free from sin and He will do just that. To gain your dignity, your self-respect, and your purpose back. Love Net

RAINBOW

Now I really want to talk about something that have really been on my mind. You know how a person grow up believing different kinds of things, such as religion for instance. I'll just talk about it from a lesser point of view using myself. When I say religion, I'm talking about something that you do repetitiously or say repetitively that have your faith standing so strong to whatever you stand firm in no matter whatever it is. I believe that we do a lot of things in our lives religiously.

People smoke religiously, eat religiously, go to church repetitiously, and shop religiously. In other words, doing and/or saying things on a regular basis. But how many of us know that it's not about religion, but it's about Salvation. Now as I was growing up I used to go to church all the time with my immediate family which was the belief in the Baptist doctrine. Later to find out that I should follow the one doctrine and that's the doctrine of Holiness because GOD is Holy. But here I learned there is a GOD. Here is where I learned to say the Our Father Prayer and the Now Lord Lay Me Down To Sleep Prayer.

Here I learned how to treat people right. Here I learned about right and wrong concerning morality, somehow I did read from the mason bible too which is another story, just to name a few. While living with my mom I remember the Jehovah Witness believers coming over our house talking about Paradise, not understanding their doctrine but I remember. There was a Sanctified church right on the side of our house. Here is where I learned how they would get up running around saying words that I didn't understand, only to find out later in life they were speaking in tongues. I was so drawn to it that I Loved going there.

They all would have white on and for some reason would appear to me to be mean which I later learned they were just a stern people. And then as I got a little older I went to Catholic Central School where before I go to class, I would have to attend mass every morning. Here is where I learned about the difference from their sacrament and the baptism sacrament. I would see individuals from our church drinking from these glasses under the white sheet, but the Catholic Church that was next to the school, as I went to mass I would see everybody drinking from the same golden looking cup that the eucharist would hold in his hand.

I never did drink from that cup as I've seen others did. I would listen to the choir and move on. But I did do the Hail Mary Full of Grace The Lord is With Thee Prayer, then off to class. And then when I was grown, here is where I learned about Jesus and the Apostle's Doctrine. Here is where I learned and understood about the different beliefs, the different types of baptisms, the Holy Bible, the order of different organizations where the voting for positions would take place, and learned what Disciple Ship was about.

I'm blessed to know a little bit of these

different kinds of groups of worlds. Most importantly I know of this great big Creator who created all living and moving things. And I do thank Him for that. With all the different kind of controversy in the world, people doing their own thing, saying it's their own body and they can do what they want, No, no, and no. Some say that there is no GOD.

Personally I have to say otherwise because I know that there is a Creator that started this beginning series of our lives. Well how is it that I come from my mom and she comes from her mom and she comes from her mom and so forth backwards to the beginning. The human had to start from somewhere. There is argue that man comes from monkeys for one. I can't understand why the monkeys that are still here today, why they haven't evolved. They argue this is a man's world for two, argue about abortions, which is the worship of the satanic people sacrificing aborted babies. Do a little study. They argue about the Bible, argue about different types of preferences, just to name a few.

Now I want to really know why is it that we can pick up all other kinds of books such as magazines, harlequin love books, different types of schools books, sex books, and don't have a problem with the majority of its contents. But when it comes to the Bible, there is so much friction. Never fail to argue not paying attention that the Living GOD is not the Author of confusion.

Most people say that man wrote the bible, ummm well yea. It has different writers but Only One Author. Just like people who have experienced some things in their lives and are inspired to write about them. Different experiences in their lives but one author of their book. Some just be like I have an idea or something to say and just began to write. And with no problem. But when it comes to the Word of GOD oooh boy they just go haywire. There is one thing I know without anybody telling me and without a shadow of a doubt and that is man can't make no water.

You need water to make Kool-Aid with, need water for baths, cooking and cleaning. I know that man didn't make the sun, moon, or the stars. Trees and animals either. Although there is the cloning business, they still need the original DNA. They say Science did it. Well if science did it, Who created science? Now this is only a start. I also know for a guaranteed fact that man is not the one who put the rainbow in the sky let alone made the sky. I personally and honestly don't have any problem with what people do with their life because I just love people period and I am not their judge and that's not my position.

That's between them and their god, but (My Purpose Is) to tell you the Truth about what's been revealed to my mind. What I have a problem with is that children grow up seeing the very things that out right defies the morals of what we know shouldn't be and are against GOD'S Law of Creation. What I'm saying on one instance is, we All know that these earthly people didn't make the rainbow in the sky and My Purpose Is to try to have you understand an event that calls for logic, common knowledge, and the obvious truth of something. If I'm wrong correct me, but If I'm correct which I know I am, it was put in the sky as a sign that the Creator wouldn't flood the earth again. I know some don't agree with the flood but to each its own. But I'm having a problem because as I believe and teach the truth to my children they see otherwise.

You have people who have the audacity to listen to the enemy whisper in their ear and in their minds that they can out right defy the Creator of all flesh to use the rainbow sign for a logo. Talking about women lying with women and men lying with men. No I have to tell you that is not what the rainbow represented. People I have to tell you that is a big trick of the devil to sell your soul to hell. Satan don't give two thirds of crap about you so long as you go with that demonic spirit. Long as you agree to whatever type of demonic spirit then the enemy is happy knowing that you're not pleasing the Almighty Creator and is on your way to fire and brimstone. Yes I know about some have been raped by the same sex but it is Still common sense that that is not the way it's supposed to be.

Just like GOD made knowing your mate as in love making but the enemy decides to teach people that let's just have sex where sex consist of all kind of ways and different sex objects being used to say the least. I've learned and still learning that everything GOD did or said that is good for His creation the enemy instilled it in men's mind to do the opposite.

Wait now I love them too as a person because I'm nobody to pass on judgement. But it bothers me. Now I must tell you that coming from the enemy who brings all these different kinds of immoralities and poisons to your mind, it is up to you to cast down everything that tries to exalt itself against the knowledge of GOD and bring your thoughts into captivity to the obedience of Christ. Put your mind on Christ. Yea I know some have a problem with Christ too the reason why it's the biggest argumentative subject. Yes I know that you have to rightly divide the Word of Truth because they have added to it and took away from it but The Word of GOD Never Changes.

I have issues as well, as you read a little earlier about me. Some I've got blessed to overcome and still working on some things. But (My Purpose Is) to overcome all things that are not of GOD and pass that little knowledge on to someone else who has or is going through these things that try to tear their soul apart. Let them know that GOD is a delivering GOD and will free you up of all the things that are ungodly. Let them know that Jesus loves them just that much that He did die for them to have Everlasting life of peace, love, and joy in Him and with Him.

Now I need you to get up off your bed, get off your couch, get off your jail cell bed, camp bed, where ever you may be and get to a mirror and look into your eyes hard and tell yourself that you are beautiful, you are somebody, you can make it, you've been knocked down long enough, it's not too late for me as long as GOD give me a chance and directs me, I Can Do This. Don't you all sit there and continue to let this darkness overtake you. I don't even know why I just start talking about this just know that You Can Come Out and Be Victorious because of the rainbow. My Purpose Is

DON'T GIVE UP

I've been saying for a long time, how am I going to tell somebody or be a witness to somebody about GODs goodness and His grace if I never been through anything. I have been through so much in my life even as a child that as I look back over my life it seems as if those things wasn't anything when in fact it was some blows that I used to say in my mind and out loud that I didn't want to be alive any more. Oh yeah I wished that I would have never said that because after I said that I felt so low like how selfish of me to have said that.

Even in the midst of differences Life has never ever dealt me anything but good, positive, and blessed as far back as I can remember because I'm alive. How dare I to say that. There has been times that death has been at my door literally a few times I could have been dead BUT GOD made the hand of stinking death behave. And besides who was I to wish such a horrible saying as that, I didn't give myself life. GOD is the life giver. Example number 1, when I was having my son at the last month, time for me to go in. I walked to the hospital being that I didn't have anyone to take me.

When I arrived at the hospital, they got me all prepped and time for delivery. By that time the baby dad and his friend Dallas had arrived. I remember hearing the staff saying that we can save the baby. At that time I didn't know exactly what they were talking about until after I knew I was given four pints of blood back into my body which at first happens to be the wrong type of blood because every time this I will never forget, my left hand is where they had the IV and my hand was swollen so big because the blood was running a little too fast even with it being as thick as it was and when they would have me to try to walk, I would pass out. But they finally got it together.

You can't give somebody a different type of blood in their veins. If they're a negative o positive you can't give them b negative blood for instance. Well that's exactly what happened to me when they gave me the four pints of blood through the transfusion of some different type that was not of my own. Talking about being sick with headaches and all, shucks GOD spared my life with this one because you just don't mess around with blood only when it's the Blood of JESUS Amen.

You know I think about the many operations that I've gone up under with the different kinds of medicines that the doctors used to put me to sleep. After a while of thinking it started to become a little fearful to the point of the body getting used to it till I said no way I'm not going to let the doctors continue to operate on me because it seems like things were starting to become regular but I was still hurting. On one hand after a while the placebo's was coming into play and on the other hand my body seems to continue to be racked with pain.

Now I'm not selfish to the point of wear and tear of child bearing and wear and tear from drugs and healing from that, and the beatings that my body took but my GOD I'm not slow to the field of game playing. Meaning the game of medicine. I'm going somewhere with this just hold on one second. I have been hit in my head with a board that had nails in it, I had a full window fall on my right arm cutting across wards ripping the muscles from it that the doctors said while they were stitching it up that I would never be able to use my hand again.

My right foot broke in three different places so bad it took them seven screws and three plates to sew it back together, and I was told I was not to wear high heels shoes again, but I do. I fell on ice at my job and cracked my tailbone where even today the x-rays show the crack is still there. These just a few things I been through as far as having to take pain killers or even fake pain killers for and need my Faith of Healing to sure nough come on in and take control. This is mi-nute to some but "My Purpose Is" to let the ones who will to take this and know that

GOD Is Your Healer and No matter what kind of Pain that comes in your life, rather if it comes by way of your mind, your physical, your social, your whatever, just know that JESUS Loves You and He Got You. I'm no preacher who gets in the pulpit because I know I can testify better than that, and besides that's not my call amen.

My Purpose Is to let you know that GOD is not respective of person, if He saved and Blessed and Healed little ole me then He can and will do it for you. Amen yes. I remember in the summer of 2009 when I was laying on the couch looking up at the ceiling, listening to everybody run in and out the house with laughter and all, that all I can do was just cough and cough and vomit.

My head was pounding so hard and I could barely move because my bones were hurting me so bad that all I could do was cry. So after some hours go by my mom comes out of her room because she hears me crying and asks me if I want her to fix me something to eat, I say yes ma'am, some of my favorite which is mushroom soup. And she did. So I made it to the kitchen table and I was real hot to the point that I was really sick. Well guess what loves, my then daughter in law Jackie and my son Michael took me to the hospital. I was so hot that I would lay on the hospital floor until they would call me to the back. They ran the test and all. They hooked me up to machines and gave me lots of fluids and things. After a while they told my daughter in law that if she'd waited an hour later that I would have died. It was just that serious because of the H1N1 Virus spreading throughout my body save a few percent.

After hours at the hospital I woke up that they gave my son this medicine for me to take, but he kept telling me not to take it. I was for once afraid. But when they let me go home, I was still vomiting, so I took the bathroom trash pail and laid on the living room floor because I knew I was about to take that medicine anyway because I wanted to get better. When I say that I never in my life saw anything so nasty in my life come out of somebody's body like this before, oh my God, when I took that medicine I threw up nothing but Black stuff that filled up half of the trash can and it was stinking so bad. My son and husband were standing there like they were going to take me back to the hospital. I said with everything I had in me, no. I take it that the black stuff was poison.

I'm talking about the things that had me saying that I didn't want to be here anymore because I was at a weak point in my life. Yes I have been through some things that were attacking my body that I myself thought that I would never come out of, not realizing that somebody was praying for me. If you're reading this I want to say thank you and I love you because I wouldn't made it without you and GOD.

There have been times where I felt so alone like didn't nobody care about me, want me, love me, or even want to be around me, when I was dealing with these things but that was ok because I had GOD all the time. Now the last thing I'm going to let you know is when I found out that I had Pancreatic Cancer. It was right after I got over from having Renal Stage 3 Kidney Problems in 2015. Yeah the body went through a thing or two. It was after I came back from my honeymoon in 2017. The month was around February I began to feel pain around my abdomen area. I kept telling my husband that my side hurt and stomach hurt. And I kept laying down and didn't want to eat anything. This was going on for months. I was losing weight.

We do this thing at our church where we greet each other with a hug and when it was time for that, as we hugged each other my Godmother even said to me, you feel alright, you feel a little thin. I let her know what was going on and she told me to take a spoon of blessed oil and I would. My hair was coming out. My daughter was getting upset when I would ask her to comb my hair and I would laugh because she almost couldn't grip it. So around September I was hurting real bad till I was throwing up really bad and my children took me to the hospital. I know y'all probably saying she sure was going to the hospital a lot, well it was some things happening to me people. And plus remember I said How can I be a witness or tell somebody how good GOD IS if I never experienced anything. No way I'm saying you have to experience these things to be a witness, but this is what I asked the Lord.

Before I could recognize, I was going through this. But anyway I went to the hospital and they took my blood and did x-rays and all and came to the conclusion that it was pancreatitis. Upon releasing me they told me to see my primary physician. In between time I ended up in the emergency room again. Upon me seeing my primary doctor even months later the other doctors prescribed me these chemo medicines because of how long I waited. I had to see an gastroenterologists, pathologists, medical oncologists, surgical oncologists,. I choose to take the chemo pills because I just didn't want to get the port put in and I said no. I said just cut it out. I thought I was going to be out of here because I started to worrying and getting my life insurance policy together. When you worry it makes your body react. I just knew I was going to die because of how sick I was. I missed so much church because of me being so sick.

My weight kept fluctuating though. And as far as my hair something said get some 100 percent mineral oil and keep it in your hair and that's what I did for that. I was afraid but kept up a front on top of praying at the same time. But yeah I knew the risk of getting it cut on because it would run my sugar level up because that is where your sugar is held but I just said GOD be with me and yeah GOD please don't let my weight fall like that but for some reason I did gain because everytime they did the surgeries seems like my body would call for sweets. So something came to my mind to just eat only All green things and that's exactly what I start doing. Only green.

Plain green bell pepper, not cooked, sweet snap peas, spinach, green apples, every and anything green I ate. Nothing sweet. Oh and I would drink bitter tea. Now I know that pancreatic cancer is a nasty demon that will take you out of here and once again I thought I only had pancreatitis until I saw the oncologist and the others that said they need to do surgery asap, but GOD allowed me to experience this demon for a reason.

There is nothing special about me. And yes I am as of November of 2019 the cancer is at slow progression but GOD is so good. Once again My Purpose Is to let you all know that you don't have to live in a world of fear, that you can do all things through Christ that strengthens you, that you don't have to be alone, that GOD will protect you, that GOD will fight you every battle, that you can gain your lost identity back, that GOD will deliver you out of circumstances, that GOD will prosper you, and most of all GOD will Love you and be there when you need Him to be. And to Christ be the Glory. I pray that you have gotten something even if it's just one thing that will help you to uplift your spirit amen. Until next time, Pray for me as I pray for you. Love Net.

ABOUT THE AUTHOR

Born April 1962 at Mount Sinai Hospital, downtown Chicago, Illinois. Was raised in Grand Rapids, MI where I learned to be obedient to my parents and learned the skills of survival. I have five beautiful children in which GOD helped me raised in the place of Muskegon, MI.

I raised them in the Beauty of Holiness where we all (me and my children) were baptized in Jesus Name at the place called Zion Apostolic Faith Church. General Education was studied at Marshall High School and Malcolm X College of Chicago, Illinois. South Middle and Catholic Central High School, both of Grand Rapids, MI.

I went to Muskegon Public Schools where I received a Certificate in Business Office Assistant. I received a Lead Teacher Certificate through High/Scope Educational Research Foundation of South Bend, Indiana. I went to Zion Bible Institute, Inc, and received an Associate's Degree in

Foundational, Standard, and Advanced Church Ministries, graduating Magna Cum Laude. Continued my studies through Zion Bible Institute, Inc., Grace Apostolic College, Inc., International Apostolic College of Grace & Truth, where the ceremony took place in Indianapolis, receiving a Bachelor's Degree of Secular and Christian Education, also graduating Magna Cum Laude. Worked as Home Health Aide, Cabinet Maker, Teacher, Bus Driver, Computer Operator, and being a Mommy.

www.ingramcontent.com/pod-product-compliance
Lightning Source LLC
Chambersburg PA
CBHW072041110526
44592CB00012B/1515